Simon's Scoop

Carolyn Sloan
Illustrated by Jim Kilmartin

Rigby

A Harcourt Achieve Imprint

www.Rigby.com
1-800-531-5015

Literacy by Design Leveled Readers: *Simon's Scoop*

ISBN-13: 978-1-4189-3670-9
ISBN-10: 1-4189-3670-7

Printed in China
3 4 5 6 7 8 985 14 13 12 11 10 09 08

CONTENTS

CHAPTER 1
THE TEXTOWN TIMES

The first time Simon Garcia went to the office of *The Textown Times*, he felt a buzz of excitement. His uncle zoomed around the office, talking on the phone and barking orders to the other reporters. Uncle Jim was the chief reporter and worked in a messy room full of people typing noisily or talking on the phone. Now and then Simon's uncle would shout, "Hey, Mack, there's a Town Hall story breaking!" or "The mayor's car has been in a crash!"

And someone named Mack ran around, calling out, "OK, hold page two!" or "Cut the baby duck story!"

Simon sat quietly, just like he'd been told to do while Uncle Jim was busy. He thought about how his uncle, a well-known newspaper reporter in town, was lucky because his work seemed to be one adventure after another.

Late in the day, the newspaper was "put to bed." This was what the reporters called it when the newspaper had gone off to be printed. After it had gone, Uncle Jim let Simon have a turn on his computer.

Simon made up a story about a local toad that became a circus clown. Uncle Jim used his computer to show Simon what his story would look like on a pretend newspaper page.

"Your boy's been quite a reporter today," Uncle Jim told Simon's mother when she came to pick him up. "He got the toad scoop for us!"

Simon wasn't sure what a scoop was, but he didn't want to ask anyone at the newspaper office. On the way home, he thought about how you used a *scoop* to serve ice cream . . . and you *scooped* up something you'd spilled on the floor.

"It means finding out about a news story before anyone else does," Mom said, "so I suppose you could *scoop* up stories."

"Well, whatever it is," said Simon, "Uncle Jim gets lots of them."

"He certainly does," laughed Mom. She was Uncle Jim's big sister, and she told Simon how he was always writing when he was a boy no older than Simon was now.

Simon thought about that a lot.

CHAPTER 2
A HUGE IDEA

Uncle Jim's office was on Simon's way home from school, and every Tuesday and Friday he went there to get a copy of the newspaper for his mother. Each time he went into the office, he felt the same excited feeling. He just *knew* that he wanted to be a real reporter when he grew up. But then he thought, "Why wait till then?"

Sometimes Simon saw his uncle, and they had a brief chat. Other times, Uncle Jim was much too busy to talk, and Simon just got a wave and a quick "Hi!"

But one day he had time to take Simon to the cafeteria for some hot chocolate. Uncle Jim said it was a "slow news day," which meant that not a lot was happening in town that day.

"I'm going to be a reporter just like you, Uncle Jim," Simon blurted out.

"Really?" his uncle said, smiling kindly.

"Yes, I want to start practicing now because Mom said you started writing when you were my age."

"So I did," laughed Uncle Jim, "and that's how you get to be a reporter. You should start young and write something every day, even if no one ever reads it."

"How do you know what to write about?" asked Simon.

"There are stories everywhere if you train your eyes and ears to find them. There are even stories in a sleepy little town like Textown," Uncle Jim offered.

"You mean I could *really* start now?" Simon asked. There was a huge idea forming inside his head.

"Well, no . . . I mean . . . yes, but . . ." Uncle Jim said. He was surprised to see Simon so excited.

"Easy now," Uncle Jim said gently. "I just want you to think about things for a minute. I suppose you think being a reporter is a bit of an adventure, don't you?"

Simon nodded quickly.

"Well, it can be hard work, too," Uncle Jim explained. "Sometimes you have to write a story over and over until it sounds just right. You want to give it color and make it come alive. And even then, the editor may not use it.

"And sometimes," he continued, "people don't tell you everything you need to know. You have to check, double check, and check again to be sure a story is true—otherwise you can get in big trouble!"

Uncle Jim's words echoed in Simon's head long after he had left *The Textown Times*. Simon got a pen out of his school bag and found a piece of paper. *There are stories everywhere . . . Write something every day . . .* But what should he write about?

CHAPTER 3

THE AMAZING RABBIT STORY

Simon's big sister Celia was nagging their mother in the kitchen the next morning. "My friend Leticia's rabbit had seven babies," she was saying, "so can we have one? Oh, please, Mom, say *yes.*" Instead, Mom said *no.*

Simon got out his new notebook. Seven baby rabbits—that was a story!

He looked up information about rabbits on the Internet during his library hour. He learned that a female is called a *doe*, a male is a *buck*, the babies are called *kits* or *kittens*, and a group of kittens is called a *litter*.

Simon started writing his rabbit story using all the facts and new words he had learned.

At the end of the school day, he found Celia's friend Leticia in front of the school and asked in a serious voice, "So your rabbit's had seven kittens?"

"No, my rabbit had baby rabbits, not kittens!" snapped Leticia.

"What are they like?" asked Simon.

"They're small and pink. And, you know, they look like baby rabbits."

"So how is she . . . the mother?" Simon struggled to think of a good question to ask.

"I don't understand what you are talking about," Leticia said. "She had babies, OK? Rabbits do it all the time. It's not that amazing."

Simon rushed home to write his story. He thought of a great headline, which would be the title of his story. It read: AMAZING RABBIT HAS SEVEN PINK BABIES!

He typed it up on the computer and printed out a clean and perfect copy. Uncle Jim would have to run his story!

"Good try," Uncle Jim said the next afternoon after he'd read the rabbit story. "But it's not quite newsworthy enough for us to run, Simon. Now if the rabbit were to have a litter of frogs . . . that would be news!"

"But I did a good job on the writing, right?" Simon asked hopefully.

"It doesn't quite come alive," said Uncle Jim. "When it comes to animal stories, we want to know what the animal looks like, feels like, and smells like. While we're reading your story, we want to feel like we're standing right there with you, looking down at the new rabbits."

"Well, I didn't exactly see them," Simon explained. "But I spoke to Leticia about them."

"Then you should have gotten a quote from her," Uncle Jim said. "Quotes let us know where you got your information from."

Uncle Jim patted Simon on the shoulder. "Don't let it get you down. This is only your first try. It takes a lot of practice to be a good writer. Don't give up on it, OK? I know one day you will be a great reporter!"

Simon was thoughtful as he left Uncle Jim's office. He was disappointed that his uncle hadn't liked his story, but he wasn't ready to give up yet. He thought of all the ways he could make his story better. With that in mind, he headed over to Leticia's house.

"I'm writing about rabbits for *The Textown Times*," Simon announced. "May I see your baby rabbits and ask a few questions?"

"You can ask, but they won't answer!" Leticia joked.

Simon looked into the rabbit hutch, which was the cage where the rabbits lived. The kittens were small and pink. Their eyes weren't open yet, and they didn't have any fur. Simon gently petted one with a finger. It was smooth and warm.

This was what Uncle Jim meant when he said he wanted to know what the kittens looked like, felt like, and smelled like. Simon wrote all of this down in his notebook.

"What else can you tell me about them?" he asked.

"Well, they're three days old, and they can't see or hear yet," Leticia said. Then she put on a silly voice and said jokingly, "Mommy bunny's very happy, and the babies are growing, and I don't have homes for them yet, and now will you go away and stop bothering me, please?"

Back at home Simon told his mom how mean Leticia had been.

"Uncle Jim's had some tough times, too, getting people to talk," Mom chuckled. "He's had dogs chase him, eggs thrown at him, and people scream at him. But he never lets it get to him. And you can't either, Simon."

Simon rewrote his rabbit story five times before he was happy with it. When he arrived at *The Textown Times* to show Uncle Jim, his uncle had gone out, so Simon explained to the news editor that he had brought his finished story back.

The news editor took a quick look at Simon's story. "Your uncle *asked* you to bring this back?"

"Yes," Simon replied. "Well, sort of."

"Sorry, Simon. Can't use it, I'm afraid," the news editor said, handing Simon's story back to him. "Give me a call when you find some real news."

CHAPTER 4

THE ABANDONED DOG STORY

Simon's disappointment over the rabbit story didn't last very long. The next day he spotted another story idea—an even better story idea! That morning as Simon and his sister Celia walked to school, he saw a dog tied up next to a tree in someone's yard. The dog was still there at the end of the day when he and Celia walked back home.

"I think that dog's been left all alone," Simon said. "I don't think its owners want it any more."

"I don't think that dog has been abandoned, Simon," Celia replied. "I bet its owners are just at work."

Simon started walking up the sidewalk to the house. "I'm going to ring the bell and . . . "

"You'll do no such thing!" said Celia, stopping him.

"Then I'll write this up and take it to *The Textown Times*, and maybe the poor thing will be rescued," Simon said, pulling out his notebook.

"You can't do that," said Celia, looking back at the dog again, "can you?"

"Uncle Jim works there, and I'm learning to be a reporter," said Simon, writing as fast as he could.

Celia read Simon's story over his shoulder and thought how sad it would be if the dog really were abandoned. "*Pitiful* has only got one *t*," she told him, pointing to his misspelling.

"Thanks." Simon fixed his mistake. "If we hurry, we can get this story in before the newspaper is put to bed!"

"Wait. Put to what?" Celia asked, but there was no time to answer. She and her brother went running down the street to *The Textown Times.*

When Celia took out her cell phone and called their mom to say where they were going, Mom didn't sound the least bit surprised.

A different news editor at *The Textown Times* said Uncle Jim was out covering a music festival.

"Can you read my story?" Simon asked her. "It's about an abandoned dog, and it's really important."

"Well, then, I suppose I'd better look at it," the editor said, grinning. She glanced at Simon's notebook, scratched her head, and said, "Hmm, I like what you have written about the dog, but you don't have the street address in here."

"Oh no!" Simon cried. "It was South Street, 22 . . . I think . . . "

"It was 24 South Street," Celia whispered.

The editor heard them and asked, "Are you sure it's 24 South Street? That's Annie Higgins's house—she's my babysitter. I didn't know they'd gotten a dog."

She turned away, picked up a phone, and dialed Annie's number. When she put the phone down, she looked grim. She knew Simon wouldn't like what she had to say.

"That dog belongs to Annie's brother, and it simply doesn't *like* being inside houses."

"Oh, really?" Simon asked, feeling bad. "But it seemed like it had been abandoned."

"*Seems* doesn't mean *is*," she explained. "You can get into trouble if you say that people are treating pets badly when they aren't!"

She turned to Celia and said, "Take him home, dear, before he does any real harm."

"Come on, Simon," said Celia, taking her brother by the arm. "And say you're sorry."

Simon was so upset that he nearly gave up his dream of being an ace reporter—but that was before another amazing scoop arrived in town.

CHAPTER 5

THE CAPTAIN COOL STORY

One day Simon was walking along the high school football field, and he could not believe what he saw. Roger Stoller was playing football with some boys from Textown's high school team! It was Roger Stoller, the famous actor who played Captain Cool on TV. But here he was, running around coaching the team as though he was just a regular guy. Simon wrote down the color of his shirt, the kind of shoes he wore, the time of day, and the fact that the sun was shining. Before Simon could get some quotes, the man jumped onto a motorcycle and roared away.

Simon went onto the field and said to the nearest player, "I'm reporting for *The Textown Times.* You guys are really lucky to have someone famous coaching you!"

The boy looked at him strangely and walked away.

"It is him, isn't it? Your coach?" Simon asked another player.

"That's our coach, sure, and he's great. So what?"

"But what . . . I mean, how . . . does he ever talk about, you know . . . Cool?" Simon stuttered.

"He's cool all right, but he just helps us win," the player replied.

Simon continued on with his questions. "Does he ever talk about . . . you know . . . TV?"

"No, and why are you asking all these questions, anyway?"

"Well, why aren't you answering my questions?" Simon asked. It was then that he knew that he was on to something big. He replied, "It's because he doesn't want anyone to know who he is, isn't it?"

One of the boys pushed toward him. "Look, kid, we've got nothing to say to any newspaper, so just leave, OK?"

Simon left, but now he was sure that he'd gotten the amazing scoop he'd been waiting for—a celebrity with a secret!

He rushed home to write his story—
with quotes and everything!

CAPTAIN COOL'S BIG SECRET!!

Something very strange is going on in Textown. The high school football team (who hasn't won a game all season) has been secretly coached by no less than Captain Cool star Roger Stoller!

"He's a great coach," said one player, "but we can't get his autograph because no one's supposed to know he's here."

Simon had made up the last part about the autograph. As he was finishing his story, he wondered why it was all so secret. Should he be telling the whole town about it? In the end, he told himself that this was what real reporters did—they reported newsworthy news.

Simon hurried to *The Textown Times* the next day and slammed his scoop down on his uncle's desk.

"Now *this* looks promising," said Uncle Jim, reading Simon's story. "You're quite sure it was Roger Stoller, Captain Cool himself? None of the players actually say it was."

"It was him, " Simon replied. "I'm sure of it."

Uncle Jim turned to another reporter, who nodded and took Simon's story away.

Simon's uncle was not happy when the reporter came back a few minutes later.

"Oh, Simon," Uncle Jim groaned, "you have to learn to check to make sure your story is true! This man may have *looked* like Roger Stoller, but he *wasn't* Roger Stoller!"

Simon hung his head. He felt awful that he'd messed up another story.

"I'm sorry," Uncle Jim went on, more gently, "but you've got to stop coming here with your wild tales, OK?"

"OK," said Simon, feeling hot tears in his eyes.

"Maybe one day you will make a good reporter, but let's just wait till you're a bit older and wiser. Sound good?"

CHAPTER 6
FRONT PAGE!

Simon didn't stop writing stories, but he did stop showing them to people. And so it might have gone on this way, had his best friend Marco not said one day, "Too bad you're not writing stuff for *The Textown Times* any more."

"I had to give it up," said Simon sadly.

"Why?"

"My sister Teresa's won the first round of a big spelling bee, that's why! The finals are going to be on TV! There's going to be someone famous in my family!"

Simon talked to Teresa, who was bubbling with excitement about her "luck," as she called it. When he got home, he wrote a story about her—and then rewrote it four times and read it through twice just to make sure it was perfect. It was newsworthy enough for *The Textown Times*, he thought. It was all true, and Teresa's quotes really made the story come alive. But Simon put the story away in a drawer with a deep sigh.

During dinner that night, Simon's mother said, "I hear Teresa has won some spelling thing and is going on TV! Anyone know where or when?"

"I've got it written down," said Simon, getting up to get his mother the story.

His mother read it with a smile growing on her face. "This is good," she said to herself. "I bet Uncle Jim . . ."

"Can I keep this to show your dad?" Mom asked aloud, and Simon nodded.

Simon was surprised the next day to find a copy of the newspaper by his plate at breakfast. He glanced at it, puzzled, then looked again. There was a photo of Teresa under the headline:

Simon started to read: "Teresa Reyes, 15, received one of the highest scores ever recorded at the National Spelling Bee in Textown. She goes on to the finals, which will be held next month and shown on TV.

'I'm delighted,' bubbly Teresa told our reporter, 'and amazed, really. But I've always found spelling quite easy—well easier than math anyway . . . '"

Simon was confused because it sounded so much like his own story. He kept reading, and at the end, a wave of joy hit him as he saw:

—*By special reporter* SIMON GARCIA.